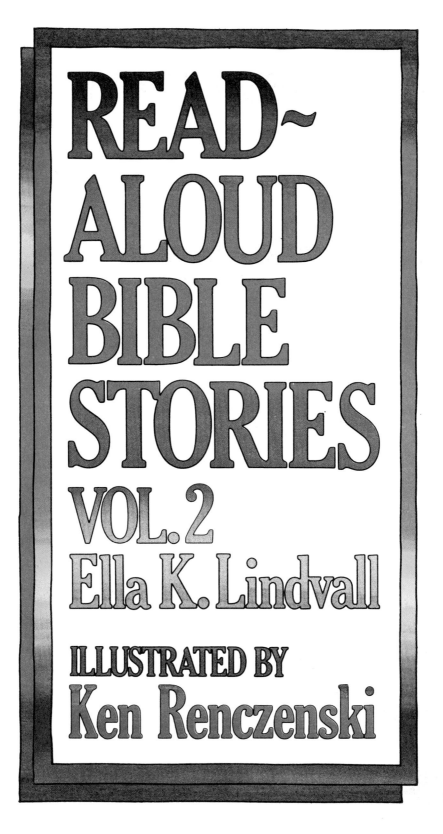

READ~ ALOUD BIBLE STORIES

VOL. 2

Ella K. Lindvall

ILLUSTRATED BY
Ken Renczenski

MOODY PRESS
CHICAGO

More stories for Jason

Moody Press, a ministry of the Moody Bible Institute, is designed for education, evangelization, and edification. If we may assist you in knowing more about Christ and the Christian life, please write us without obligation: Moody Press, c/o MLM, Chicago, Illinois 60610.

Library of Congress Cataloging-in-Publication Data
(Revised for vol.2)

Lindvall, Ella K.
    Read aloud Bible stories.

    Vol. 2 illustrated by Ken Renczenski.
    Contents: v. 1. The man who was too little. The man who couldn't see. The boys and girls and Jesus. The wind that obeyed. The man who said, "thank you" — v. 2. Simon and his boat. The boy who went away. The boy who shared his lunch. The man who helped. A sad day and a happy day.
    1. Bible stories, English.   2. Bible stories — N.T.
I. Renczenski, Ken, ill.   II. Title.
BS551.2.L48   1982   220.9'505   82-2114
ISBN 0-8024-7163-3 (v. 1)
ISBN 0-8024-7164-1 (v. 2)

Printed in the United States of America

Contents

Simon and His Boat

(Luke 5:1-11)

Simon had a boat.
Every day
Simon got
into his boat
and went
splish splash
out into the water
to catch fish.

One time Simon
and his friends
worked hard all night
trying to catch fish.
Do you know how many
they caught?

9

NOT EVEN ONE.
"Let's go home,"
they said.
So Simon
and his friends
took back
the boat
splish splash
and put it away.

After a while
step, step, step
Jesus came along.
Now EVERYBODY
wanted to get
close to Jesus.
Big people
pushed this way.
Little people
pushed that way.
There was so much
PUSHING—

that Jesus got
into Simon's boat.
"Simon," He said,
"please move
your boat
out into the water.
I want to sit in it
and talk
to the people."

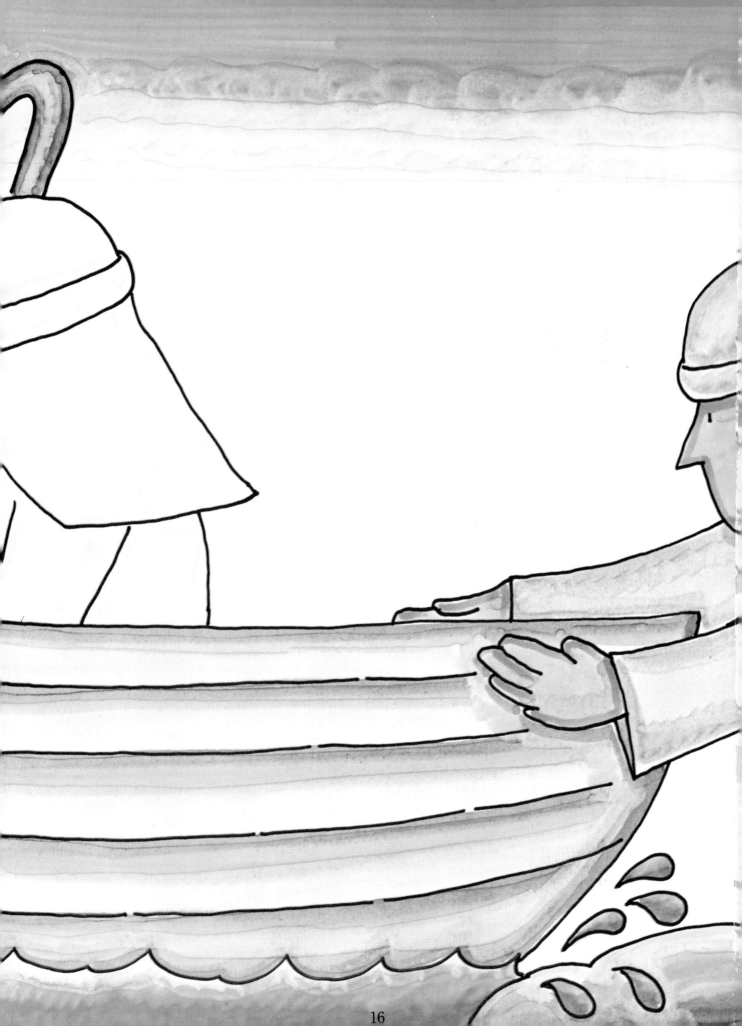

Well, Simon wanted
to please Jesus.
So he did
what Jesus said.
He pushed his boat
splish splash
out into the water.

Jesus sat in the boat. The people stood beside the water. Now everybody could see Jesus. Everybody could hear Him. Then Jesus talked to them about God.

When He was
done talking,
Jesus said, "Simon,
take your boat
out into the deep water
to catch some fish."

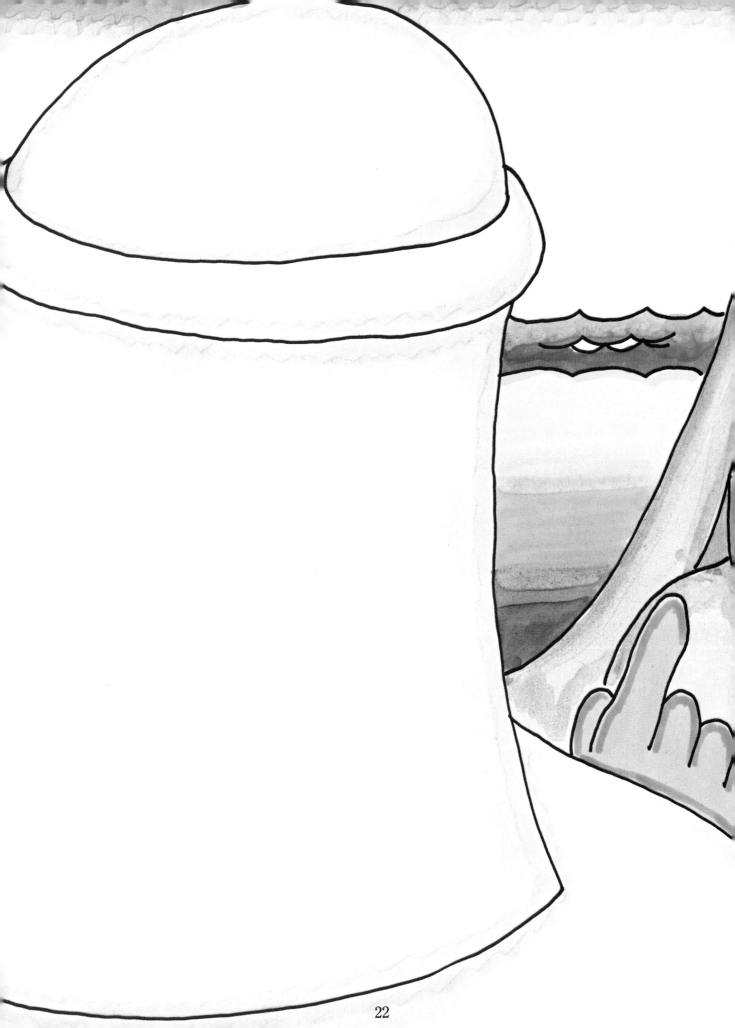

Now Simon wanted
to please Jesus,
so he said,
"We worked hard
all night to catch fish.
We didn't catch
even one.
BUT—

23

I'LL DO WHAT YOU
SAY." So Simon
made the boat
go out where
the water was deep.
His brother went, too.
They put their
fishing net
into the water.
And all at once—

24

the net was
FULL of fish.
Big fish.
Little fish.
Wiggily fish.
Oh, my!
Simon and his
brother waved to
their friends.
"Quick!
Come and help!"

The friends came
in their boat.
They filled up
both boats with fish—
big fish, little fish,
wiggily fish.
Oh, my!

Simon and his friends
looked at all
those fish.
Where had so many fish
come from?
Then Jesus told them
about something
better than
catching fish.

"From now on,"
Jesus said,
"you will
bring people
to Me."
So Simon
and his friends
left the fish.
They left the boats.
And they went
with Jesus.

What did you learn?

Simon wanted to
please Jesus.
He did just
what Jesus said.
Do YOU want
to please Jesus?
Then what
will you do?

The Boy Who Went Away

(Luke 15:11-24)

A big boy lived
with his brother
and his daddy.
The big boy
was not happy.
He didn't want
his daddy
to tell him
what to do.
So one day—

the big boy took
all his pennies
and said, "Good-bye."
Then he went FAR
AWAY down the road.

NOW his daddy
couldn't tell him
what to do.
NOBODY told him
what to do.

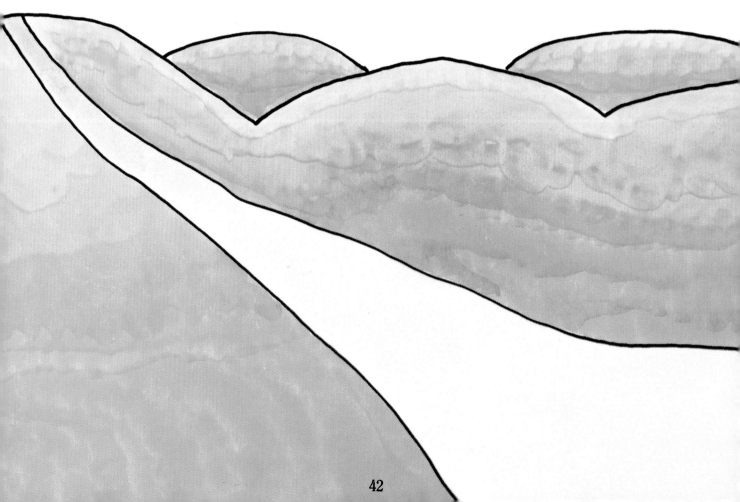

43

Nobody said,
"Eat your carrots," or,
"Don't DO that," or,
"It's time
to go to bed."
The big boy
did just what
he wanted to do.
Every day.

He took his pennies
to the store.
He bought just
what he wanted.
He had lots of fun
until one day—

his pennies were
all gone.
"I know what to do,"
the big boy said.
"I'll work.
Then I'll get
more pennies."

So he worked.
He took care of
a man's pigs.
But he never
got enough pennies.
He was hungry.
Every day.

At last the big boy
thought,
*The men who work
for my daddy—
they have lots to eat.
I'll go home
to my daddy.*

I'll say to him,
"Daddy, I've been bad.
I haven't pleased God.
I haven't pleased you.
I'm sorry."

So the big boy
started walking.
Step, step, step
went his feet.
*Step, step,
step, step*
all the way home.

His daddy
saw him coming.
His daddy ran
and put his arms
around him
and gave him a kiss.

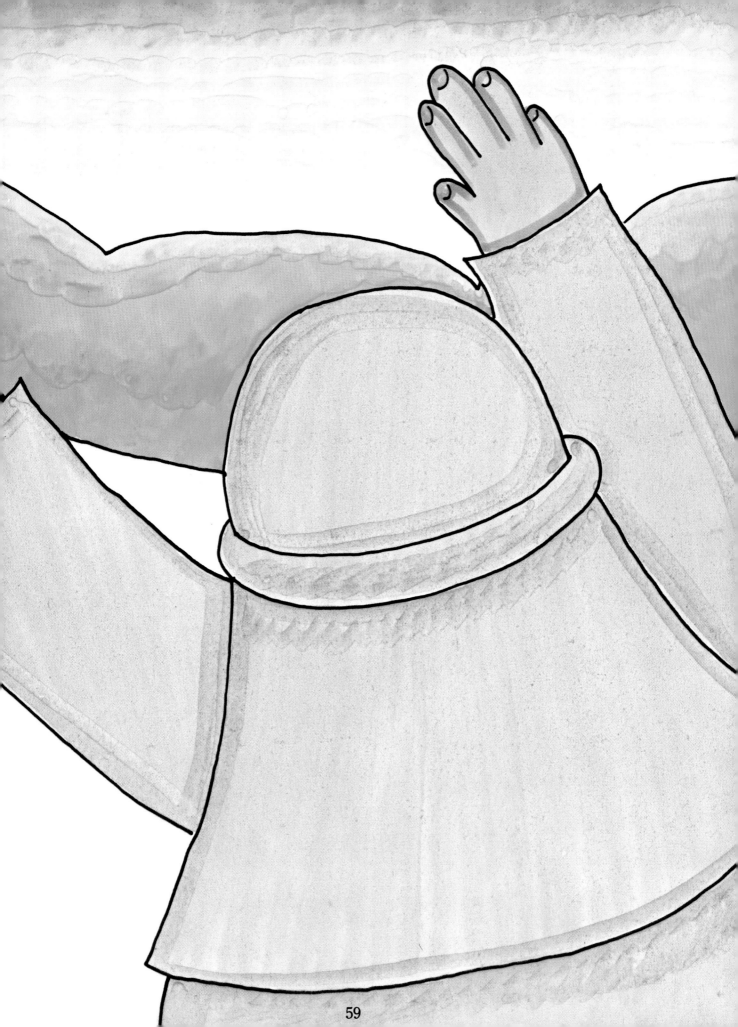

"Daddy," said the big boy,
"I've been bad.
I haven't pleased God.
I haven't pleased you.
I'm sorry."

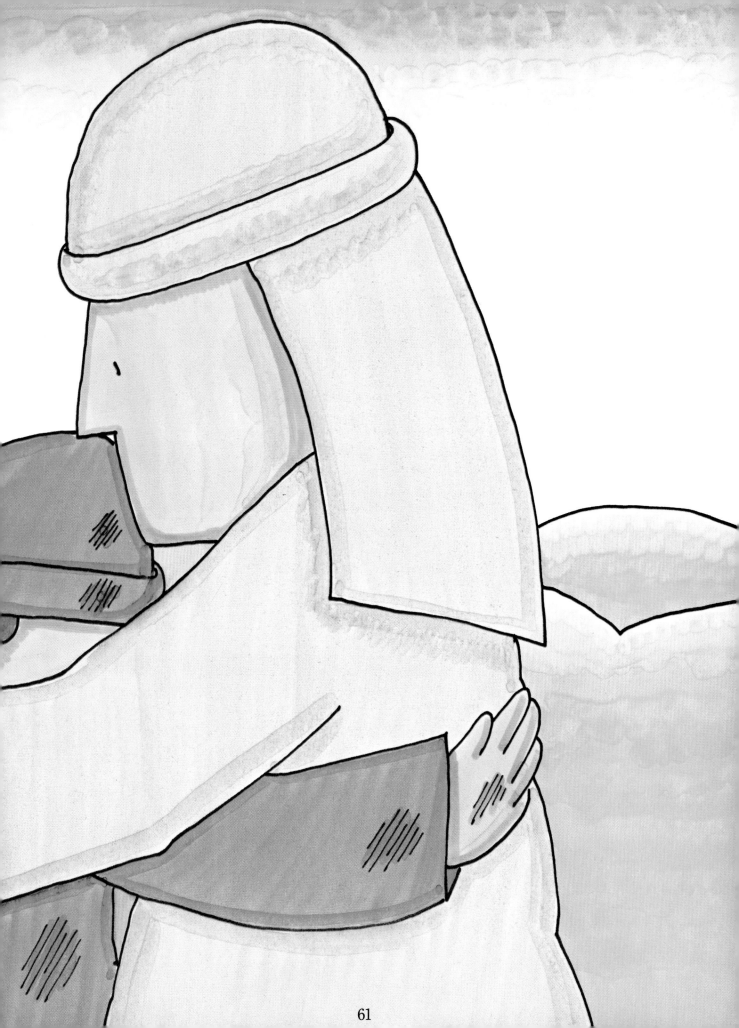

His daddy wasn't angry.
Oh, no.
His daddy said,
"Quick! Bring my boy
some new clothes!

Bring him shoes!
Bring him a ring!
My boy
has come home!
Let's have a
big dinner!"
And they did.

What did you learn?

When the boy came home,
his daddy was glad.
And when you say,
"God, I haven't pleased You.
But I'm sorry,"
that makes God
glad, too.

The Boy Who Shared
His Lunch

(Matthew 14:14-21; Mark 6:34-44;
Luke 9:10-17; John 6:1-11)

Up, up, up went Jesus,
up the big hill.
Up, up, up went
Jesus' friends,
up the big hill.

Up, up, up the big hill
went lots of people—
big people, little people,
fat people, thin people,
sick people, well people.
Boys and girls, too.

Jesus saw
the people coming.
He said hello to them.
He made the sick ones
better.
Then He talked to them
about God.
Maybe He said,
"People, God is kind.
He is your Friend."

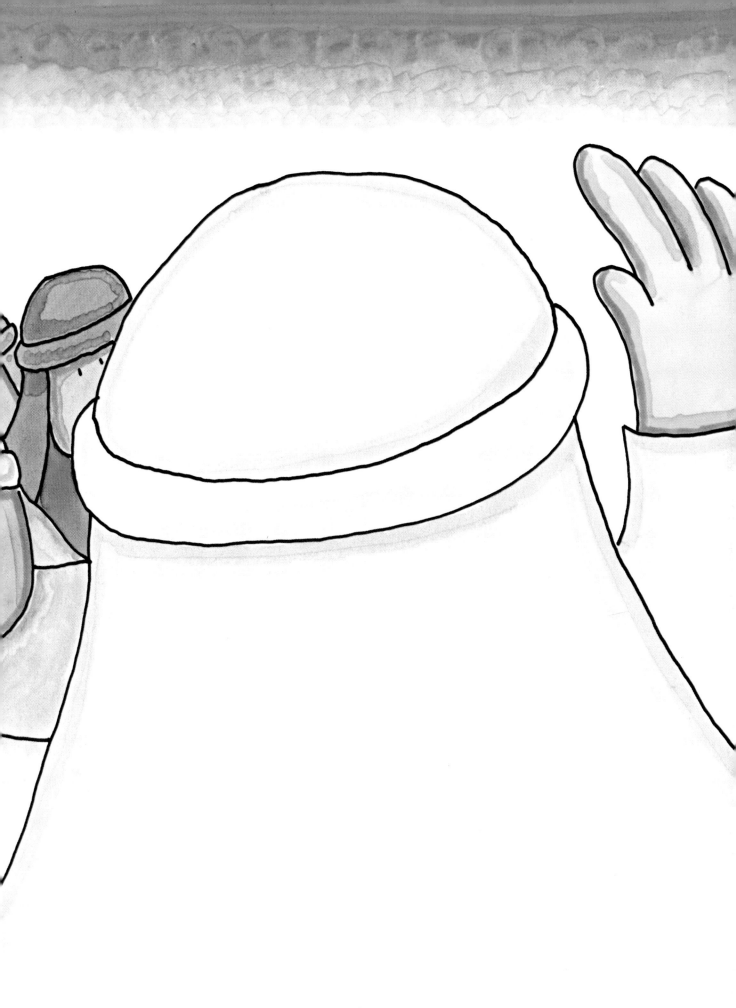

Jesus talked
for a long time.
After a while
the boys and girls
started to get hungry.
The daddies
and mommies
started to get hungry.

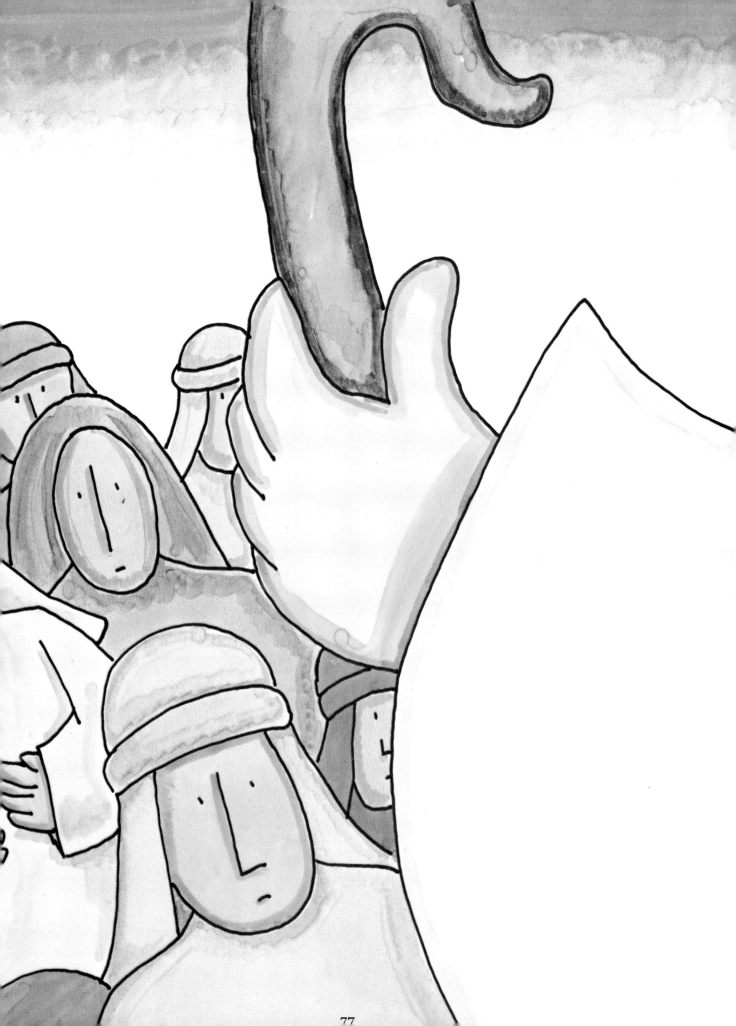

Jesus' friends said,
"Soon it will be dark.
Tell the people to go
and buy something
for their dinner."

But Jesus said,
"YOU give them
something to eat."

"Us?" said His friends. "Do you want us to go and buy food for ALL THESE PEOPLE?"

"How much bread is there?" Jesus asked. "Go and see."

His friends looked.
They said, "A boy here
has five little rolls
and two little fish.
But THAT'S not enough."

Jesus told them,
"Bring the bread
and fish to Me."
_____(child's name),
do you think that boy
let Jesus
have his LUNCH?

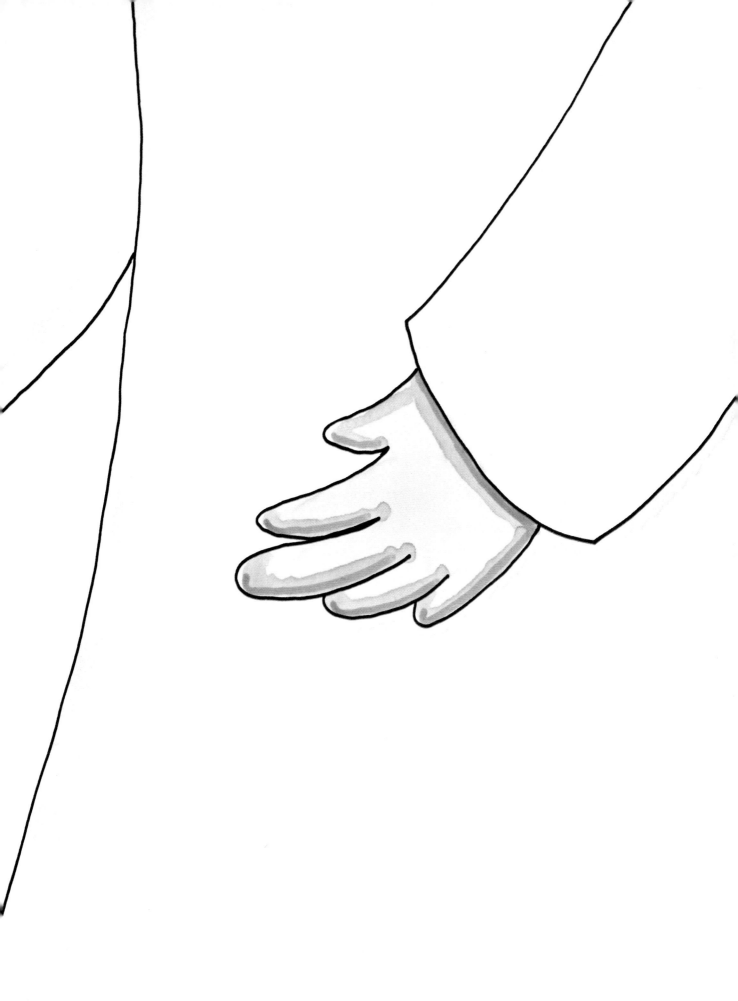

Well, he did.
All of it.
One, two, three,
four, five
little rolls
and two fish.
Do you think
Jesus said,
"Thank you"?

We know He said,
"Thank You," to God.
After that
He broke the bread.
He made it grow
into more bread.
He broke the fish.
He made them grow
into more fish.

Jesus' friends helped.
They gave bread
and fish
to everybody.
The little boy
got some, too.
And THEN—

everybody ate
bread and fish
till nobody wanted
to eat another bite.
Not even
the little boy.

What did you learn?

Jesus made
one, two, three,
four, five
little rolls
and two fish into
enough food
for lots of people.
Jesus is strong.
Jesus is kind.
Jesus is your friend.

The Man Who Helped

(Luke 10:30-37)

Down and around. Down and around. Down and around. A man was walking down a big hill all by himself.

Some bad men
saw him coming.
They hit him.
They took his pennies.
They took his clothes.
Then they ran away.

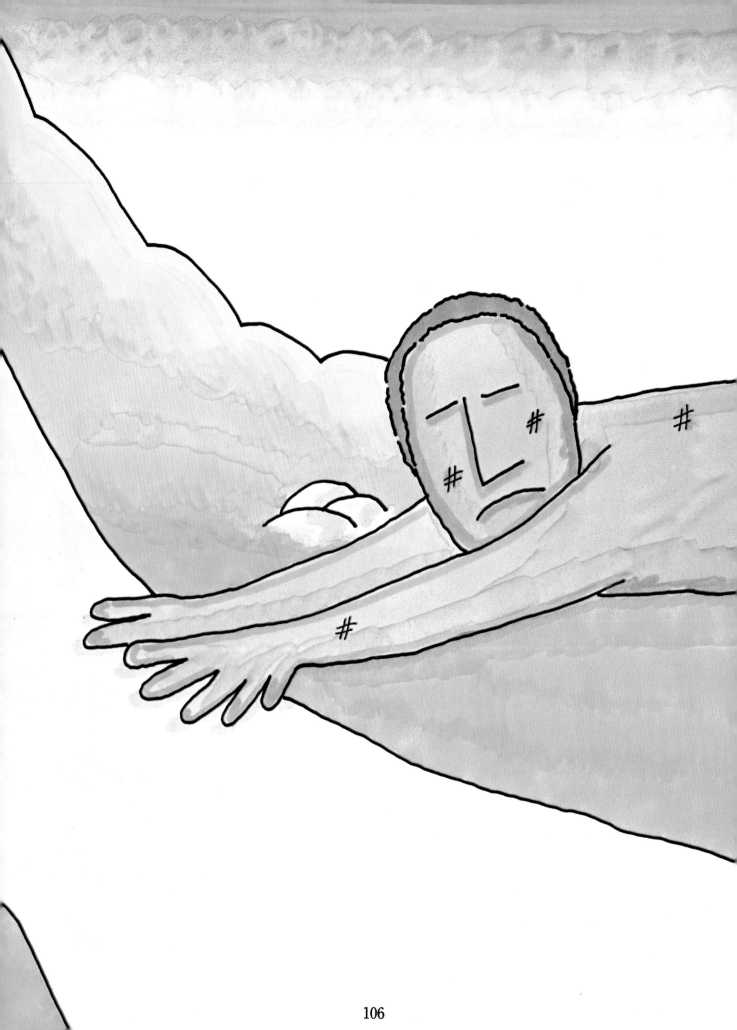

The man felt sick.
He couldn't get up.
He needed help.
Who would help?

Just then—listen—
 step, step,
 step, step.
Somebody was coming
down the hill.
Would that somebody
help?

No.
He saw the hurt man,
but he didn't
even stop.

After a while — listen—
step, step,
step, step.
Somebody else was
coming
down the hill.
Would THAT
somebody help?

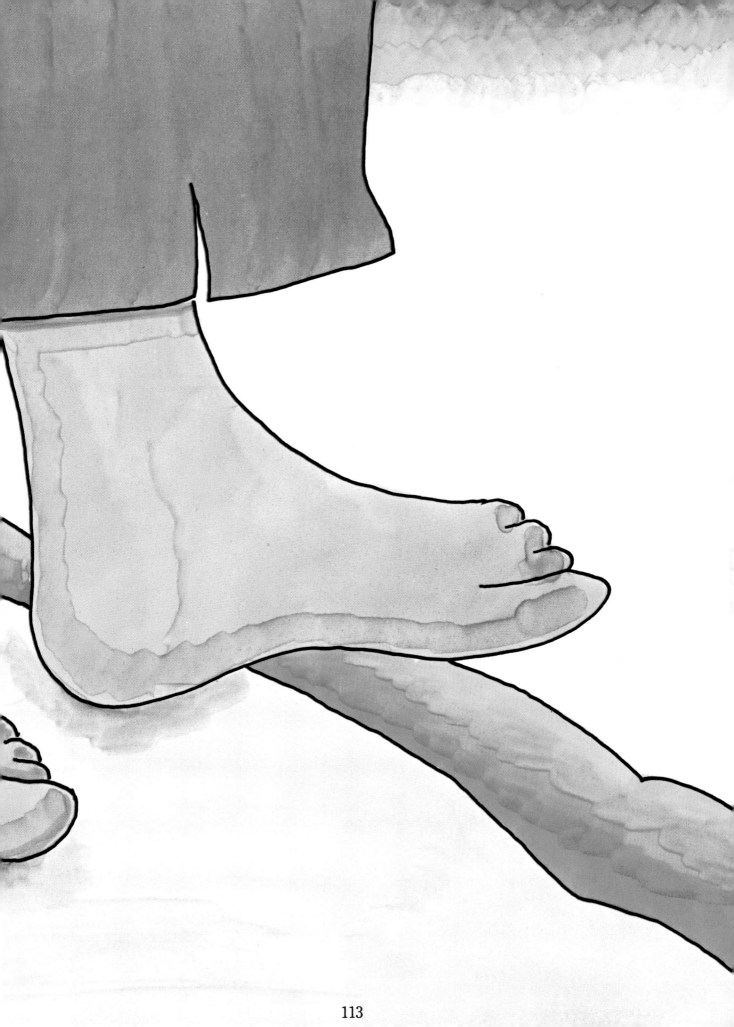

No.
He saw the hurt man,
but he didn't
even stop.

And then—what was that?—

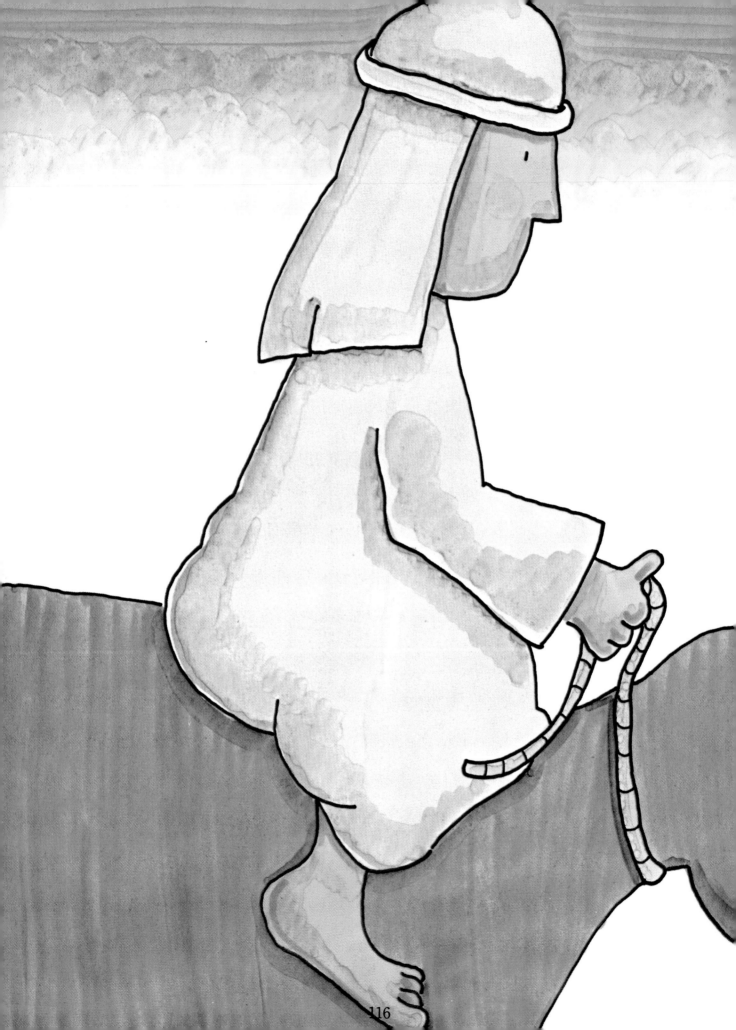

*clip, clop,
clip, clop.*
A man
and his donkey
were coming
down the hill.
Would the man
with the donkey
help?

YES.
When he saw
the hurt man
he stopped.
He helped.
He put medicine
on all
the hurt places.

He put
the hurt man
up on the donkey.
And then
they went
  clip, clop,
  clip, clop
on down
the hill.

They stopped
at a house.
The hurt man
went to bed.
The man
with the donkey
took care of him
all night
long.

In the morning
he talked
to the man
who lived there.
"I must go now.
Here are
some pennies.
Take care of him
till he
is better."

Then he got
on his donkey
and went
  clip, clop,
  clip, clop,
  clip, clop
down the road.

What did you learn?

The man with the donkey
was a helper.
The Lord Jesus wants
YOU to be a helper.
When somebody
needs help,
what will you do?

A Sad Day and a Happy Day
(Matthew 28:1-10; Mark 16:1-8)

What a sad day!
Bad men didn't
like Jesus.
They put Him
on a cross.
And He died.

What a sad day!
Jesus' friends
wrapped Him up.
They took Him
to a place
called a "tomb."
The door
of the tomb
was a big stone.

What a sad day!
Jesus' friends
went home.
They couldn't be
with Jesus anymore.
They couldn't talk to
Jesus anymore.

What a sad day!
Some ladies said,
"We loved Jesus, too.
Let's go and see
the place where
they put Him."

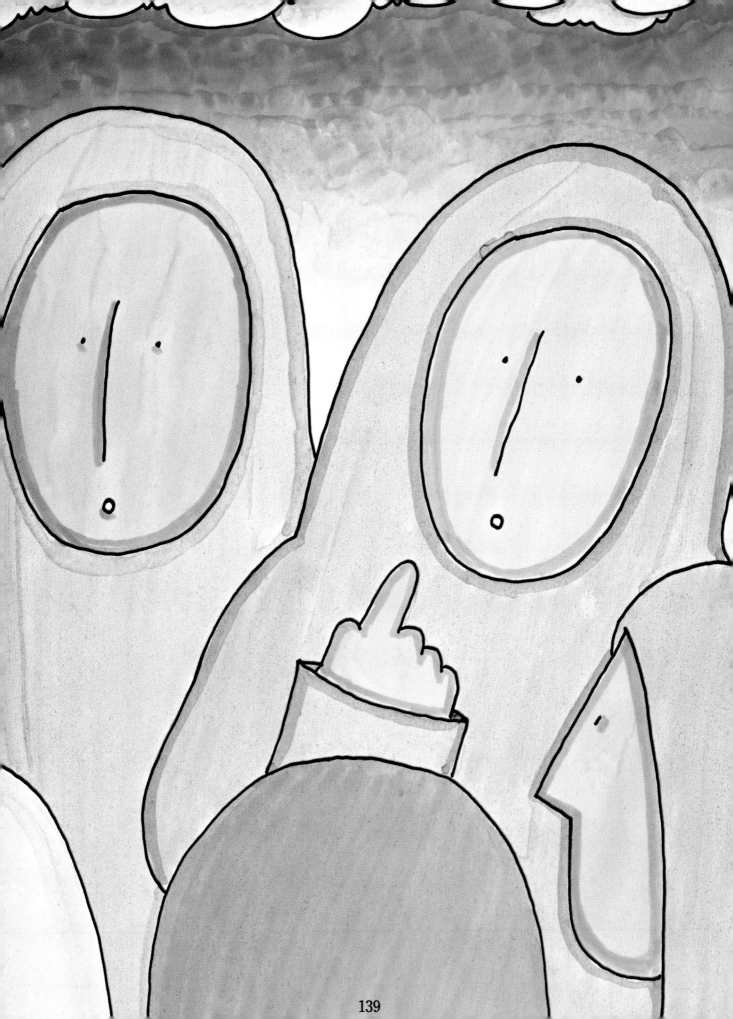

So the ladies went
walking and talking
down the road.
They said,
"Who will move
the big stone
so we can get in?"
But when
they got there—

the big stone
was rolled away
from the door place.
One of God's angels
had moved it.

The ladies went inside.
They looked this way.
Jesus wasn't there.
They looked that way.
Jesus wasn't there.
And then—

they saw an angel.
"Don't be afraid,"
the angel said.
"Don't be afraid.

"I know you are
looking for Jesus.
He's not here.
He's not dead anymore.
Go tell His friends.
Jesus is alive."

Well, the ladies
WERE afraid.
But they
were happy, too.
(Run, ladies! Run fast!
Tell Jesus' friends!)
Away they went.
What a happy day!

Away they went.
And Jesus met them.
"Good morning,"
He said.
The ladies stopped.
They looked at Jesus.
They touched Him.
He WAS alive.
What a happy day!

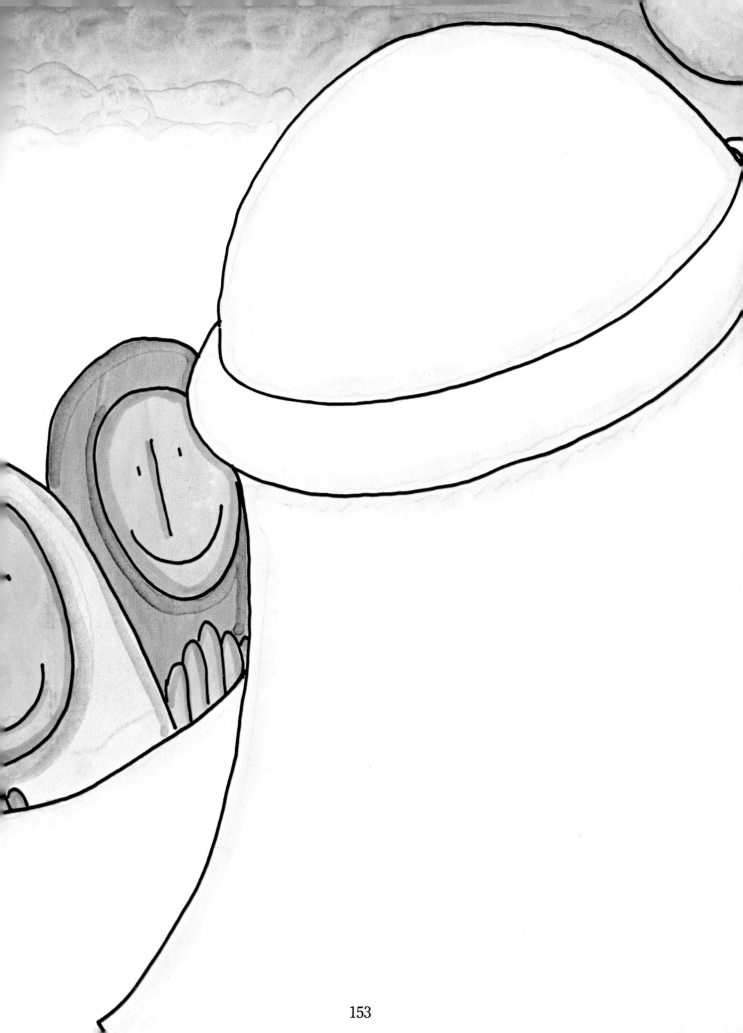

"Don't be afraid,"
He said.
"Go and tell
My friends
that I am alive
and that they
will see Me."

What a happy day!
The ladies ran.
They ran fast.
They ran to tell
Jesus' friends:
"He's alive.
We saw Him!
He's alive!"

157

What did you learn?

God made Jesus
alive again.
The ladies saw Him.
They were glad.
You and I
haven't seen Jesus.
But He is with us.
We can talk to Him.
Every day.
And that makes
US glad.